Words of Wis

A Daily Book of Inspi

Compiler's F

As I sit down to write this foreword for "Words of Wisdom: A Daily Book of Inspirational Quotations," I am overwhelmed with a sense of gratitude and reflection. Life has a way of presenting us with unexpected challenges and hurdles, and it is during these moments that we often seek solace and guidance from various sources.

For me, inspirational quotes have been a constant source of strength, reminding me of the indomitable human spirit and the power we possess within ourselves.

Like many of us, I have encountered numerous roadblocks and moments of self-doubt over the years. There were times when I questioned my abilities and the path I had chosen.

It was during one such period of uncertainty that I stumbled upon a quote that resonated with me deeply: "The only limit to our realization of tomorrow will be our doubts of today." These profound words by Franklin D. Roosevelt are the first inspirational quote in this book.

They were also the words that ignited a fire within me, propelling me to cast aside my doubts and forge ahead with renewed determination.

Inspirational quotes possess a unique ability to capture the essence of human emotions and experiences in just a few words. They distill wisdom, hope, and encouragement into concise expressions that can profoundly impact our lives.

When we encounter a quote that speaks directly to our hearts, it has the power to shift our perspective, rekindle our passions, and inspire us to take action.

As I delved deeper into the realm of motivational quotes, I discovered an endless treasure trove of wisdom. Quotes from great minds like Mahatma Gandhi, Mark Twain and Shakespeare, along with proverbs and enlightening words from philosophers, became my guiding lights, illuminating my path when it seemed darkest.

Each quote served as a beacon of hope, reminding me that even in the face of adversity, there is always a silver lining, a lesson to be learned, and an opportunity for growth.

In "Words of Wisdom: A Daily Book of

Inspirational Quotations," you will find a carefully curated collection of inspirational and motivational quotes, handpicked with the intention of empowering you on your own journey of self-discovery and personal growth.

Whether you are seeking guidance during challenging times, looking for inspiration to pursue your dreams, or simply in need of a gentle reminder of your inner strength, this book will serve as your faithful companion.

There is one quote for every day of the year and each quote is backed by a similarly inspirational photograph.

When used properly these quotes are much more than just words on a page, they can become catalysts for personal transformation. So as you immerse yourself in the pages of this book, approach each quote with an open mind and an open heart.

As a parting message, I will leave a quote that has stuck with me over the years and changed my attitude toward life:

“If something won’t matter in 5 years, don’t waste more than 5 minutes worrying about it now.”

Remember in 100 years' time no one reading this will still be around. That is why most things in life that seem important actually don't matter too much. Just make the most of your time with those people around you that you care about.

Good luck!

Steve Mandaluff

JANUARY 1

"The only limit to our realization of tomorrow will be our doubts of today."

FRANKLIN D. ROOSEVELT

JANUARY 2

Confidence is not walking into a room thinking you are better than everyone; it's walking in and not having to compare yourself to anyone at all."

UNKNOWN

JANUARY 3

"The moment you're ready to quit is usually the moment right before a miracle happens. Don't give up."

UNKNOWN

JANUARY 4

"The best time to plant a tree was 20 years ago. The second best time is now."

CHINESE PROVERB

JANUARY 5

"The future depends on what you do today."

MAHATMA GANDHI

JANUARY 6

"Hard work beats talent when talent doesn't work hard, but if talent works hard, it becomes unbeatable."

UNKNOWN

JANUARY 7

"Contentment is not the fulfillment of what you want, but the realization of how much you already have."

UNKNOWN

JANUARY 8

"Knowing yourself is the beginning of all wisdom."

ARISTOTLE

JANUARY 9

"Do not let yesterday use up too much of today."

NATIVE AMERICAN PROVERB

JANUARY 10

"Your mind is a powerful thing. When you fill it with positive thoughts, your life will start to change."

UNKNOWN

JANUARY 11

"Set a goal that makes you want to jump out of bed in the morning."

UNKNOWN

JANUARY 12

"Good people keep walking whatever happens. They do not speak vain words and are the same in good fortune and bad."

BUDDHA

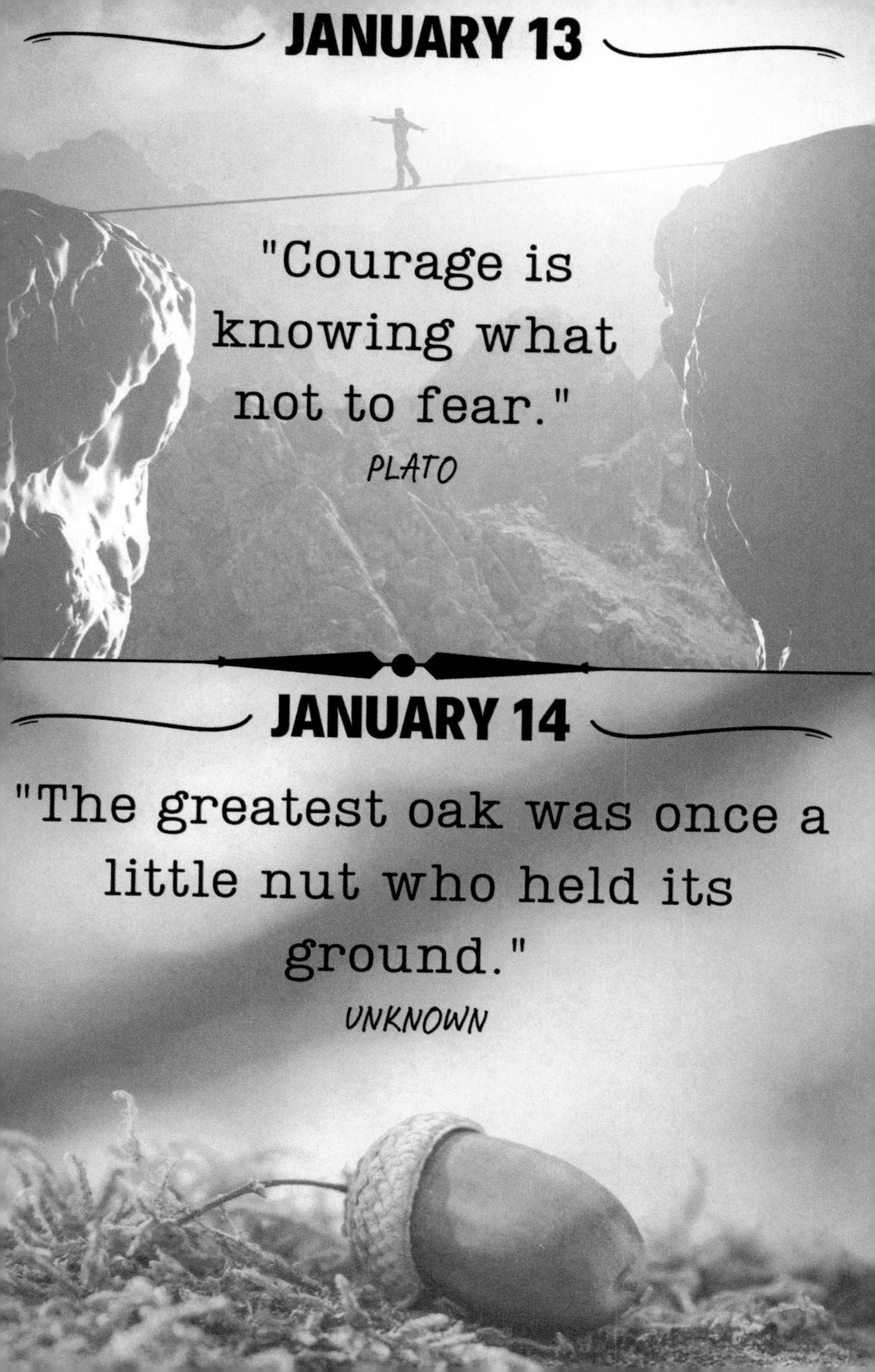
JANUARY 13
"Courage is knowing what not to fear."
PLATO
JANUARY 14
"The greatest oak was once a little nut who held its ground."
UNKNOWN

JANUARY 15

"Confidence is the key. If you don't believe in yourself, then nobody will."

UNKNOWN

JANUARY 16

"A kind word warms for three winters."

ANCIENT PROVERB

JANUARY 17

"A positive mindset brings positive things."

UNKNOWN

JANUARY 18

"The greatest inspiration you can ever get is to know that you are an inspiration to others."

UNKNOWN

JANUARY 19

"Courage is not the absence of fear, but rather the assessment that something else is more important than fear."

UNKNOWN

JANUARY 20

"You gain strength, courage, and confidence by every experience in which you really stop to look fear in the face."

ELEANOR ROOSEVELT

JANUARY 21

"The only true wisdom is in knowing you know nothing."

SOCRATES

JANUARY 22

"Perseverance is the strength within you that keeps you going when everyone else expects you to quit."

UNKNOWN

JANUARY 23

“True strength is keeping everything together when everyone expects you to fall apart."

UNKNOWN

JANUARY 24

"Fall seven times, stand up eight."

JAPANESE PROVERB

JANUARY 25

"Courage is resistance to fear, mastery of fear—not absence of fear."

MARK TWAIN

JANUARY 26

"Empowerment is not about giving people power. It's about reminding them that they already have it."

UNKNOWN

JANUARY 27

"The greatest gift you can give someone is the inspiration to achieve their full potential."

UNKNOWN

JANUARY 28

"The soul becomes dyed with the color of its thoughts."

MARCUS AURELIUS

JANUARY 29

"A journey of a thousand miles begins with a single step."

ANCIENT PROVERB

JANUARY 30

"Your words and actions have the power to inspire others. Choose them wisely."

UNKNOWN

JANUARY 31

"Life is about improvement, not perfection."

UNKNOWN

FEBRUARY 1

"Don't wait for extraordinary opportunities. Seize common occasions and make them great."

ORISON SWETT MARDEN

FEBRUARY 2

"Freedom is the only worthy goal in life. It is won by disregarding things that lie beyond our control."

EPICTETUS

FEBRUARY 3

"A lot of people tried to remove the Lone Ranger's mask. Tonto never tried."

UNKNOWN

FEBRUARY 4

"Remember, as long as you are breathing it is never too late to start a new beginning."

UNKNOWN

FEBRUARY 5

"An army of sheep led by a lion would defeat an army of lions led by a sheep."

ARABIC PROVERB

FEBRUARY 6

"The purpose of life is not to be happy. It is to be useful, to be honorable, to be compassionate, to have it make some difference that you have lived and lived well"

RALPH WALDO EMERSON

FEBRUARY 7

"Don't let the ugly in others kill the beauty in you."

UNKNOWN

FEBRUARY 8

"Some of the best days of your life haven't even happened yet. Just relax and keep going."

UNKNOWN

FEBRUARY 9

"There is only one way to avoid criticism: do nothing, say nothing, and be nothing."

ARISTOTLE

FEBRUARY 10

"Do not fear to be eccentric in opinion, for every opinion now accepted was once eccentric."

ANCIENT PROVERB

FEBRUARY 11

"People are always going to talk about you, no matter what you do. So you might as well do whatever brings you joy and live your best life."

UNKNOWN

FEBRUARY 12

"Learn from everyone. Follow no one."

UNKNOWN

FEBRUARY 13

"It does not matter how slowly you go as long as you do not stop."

CONFUCIUS

FEBRUARY 14

"The measure of a man is what he does with power."

PLATO

FEBRUARY 15

"Some people succeed because they are destined to, but most people succeed because they are determined to."

UNKNOWN

FEBRUARY 16

"Surround yourself with people who would mention your name in a room full of opportunities."

UNKNOWN

FEBRUARY 17

"Do not grieve. Misfortunes will happen to the wisest and best of men."

NATIVE AMERICAN PROVERB

FEBRUARY 18

"Whether you think you can or you think you can't, you are right."

HENRY FORD

FEBRUARY 19

"You cannot lose if you never quit."

UNKNOWN

FEBRUARY 20

"Live your life, take chances, be crazy. Don't wait, because right now is the oldest you've ever been and the youngest you'll ever be again."

UNKNOWN

FEBRUARY 21

"It is not living that matters, but living rightly."

SOCRATES

FEBRUARY 22

"Those who wish to sing always find a song."

SWEDISH PROVERB

FEBRUARY 23

"Positive vibes create positive lives."

UNKNOWN

FEBRUARY 24

"The strongest people make time to help others, even if they are struggling with their own problems."

UNKNOWN

FEBRUARY 25

"Positive anything is better than negative nothing."

ELBERT HUBBARD

FEBRUARY 26

"No one ever steps in the same river twice."

HERACLITUS

FEBRUARY 27

"One day you will tell your story of how you've overcome what you're going through now, and it will become part of someone else's survival guide."

UNKNOWN

FEBRUARY 28

"When you can't find the sunshine, be the sunshine!"

UNKNOWN

FEBRUARY 29

"The glory is not in never falling, but in rising every time we fall."

ANCIENT PROVERB

MARCH 1

"Life always offers you a second chance, it is called tomorrow."

DYLAN THOMAS

MARCH 2

"Forget the mistake, remember the lesson."

UNKNOWN

MARCH 3

"Surround yourself with those who see greatness within you."

UNKNOWN

MARCH 4

"We are what we repeatedly do. Excellence, then, is not an act but a habit."

ARISTOTLE

MARCH 5

"A heart with no dreams is like a bird with broken wings."

NATIVE AMERICAN PROVERB

MARCH 6

"When you see something beautiful in someone, speak it."

UNKNOWN

MARCH 7

"Two things to remember in life: Take care of your thoughts when you are alone and take care of your words when you are with others."

UNKNOWN

MARCH 8

"Where there is love, there is life."

MAHATMA GANDHI

MARCH 9

"The secret of happiness, you see, is not found in seeking more, but in developing the capacity to enjoy less."

SOCRATES

MARCH 10

"Enjoy the little things for one day you may look back and realize they were the big things."

UNKNOWN

MARCH 11

"Silence and a smile are two powerful tools. A smile is the way to solve many problems and silence is the way to avoid many problems."

UNKNOWN

MARCH 12

"Never trust the man who tells you all his troubles, but keeps from you all his joys."

JEWISH PROVERB

MARCH 13

"We see as we are."

BUDDHA

MARCH 14

"Reset, restart, refocus as many times as you need to. Just don't quit."

UNKNOWN

MARCH 15

"Leadership is not about being in the spotlight. It is about shining the spotlight on others."

UNKNOWN

MARCH 16

"Be kind, for everyone you meet is fighting a hard battle."

PLATO

MARCH 17

"Do not fear going forward slowly; fear only to stand still."

ANCIENT PROVERB

MARCH 18

"Forgiveness is not about forgetting, it is about letting go of the pain."

UNKNOWN

MARCH 19

"A word of encouragement during a failure is worth more than an hour of praise after success."

UNKNOWN

MARCH 20

"I have not failed. I've just found 10,000 ways that won't work."

THOMAS EDISON

MARCH 21

"Waste not fresh tears over old griefs."

EURIPIDES

MARCH 22

"Your energy is currency. Spend it well. Invest it wisely."

UNKNOWN

MARCH 23

"One smile can start a friendship. One word can end a fight, One look can save a relationship. One person can change your life."

UNKNOWN

MARCH 24

"Better a diamond with a flaw than a pebble without."

ANCIENT PROVERB

MARCH 25

"The real voyage of discovery consists not in seeking new landscapes, but in having new eyes."

MARCEL PROUST

MARCH 26

"Every day be thankful for nights that turned into mornings, friends that turned into family, dreams that turned into reality and likes that turned into love."

UNKNOWN

MARCH 27

"Don't wait for things to get better, life will always be complicated. Learn to be happy right now, otherwise you will run out of time."

UNKNOWN

MARCH 28

"Without friends, no one would choose to live, though he had all other goods."

ARISTOTLE

MARCH 29

"Words have no wings, but they can fly many thousands of miles."

KOREAN PROVERB

MARCH 30

"Before you speak ask yourself three questions: Is it true? Is it necessary? Is it kind?"

UNKNOWN

MARCH 31

"Don't compare your life to others. There is no comparison between the sun and the moon, yet they shine when it's their time."

UNKNOWN

APRIL 1

"Adversity has the effect of eliciting talents which, in prosperous circumstances, would have lain dormant."

HORACE

APRIL 2

"The more one knows, the more one realizes how little one knows."

SOCRATES

APRIL 3

"If you keep one hand on your past and one hand on your future, you'll never have either. To embrace tomorrow you must let go of yesterday."

UNKNOWN

APRIL 4

"Forgiveness is not about forgetting, it is about letting go of the pain."

UNKNOWN

APRIL 5

"To know the road ahead, ask those coming back."

ANCIENT PROVERB

APRIL 6

"No act of kindness, no matter how small, is ever wasted."

AESOP

APRIL 7

"Your mindset determines your reality. If you believe you can, you will."

UNKNOWN

APRIL 8

"Weak people seek revenge. Strong people forgive. Intelligent people ignore."

UNKNOWN

APRIL 9

"Well begun is half done."

ARISTOTLE

APRIL 10

"He who hurries cannot walk with dignity."

ANCIENT PROVERB

APRIL 11

"Make your heart the most beautiful thing about you."

UNKNOWN

APRIL 12

"Satisfy your soul, not society."

UNKNOWN

APRIL 13

"The greatest danger for most of us is not that our aim is too high and we miss it, but that it is too low and we reach it."

MICHELANGELO

APRIL 14

"He who is not a good servant will not be a good master."

PLATO

APRIL 15

"Your vibe attracts your tribe."

UNKNOWN

APRIL 16

"Whoever is trying to bring you down is already below you."

UNKNOWN

APRIL 17

"Dig the well before you are thirsty."

ASIAN PROVERB

APRIL 18

"The wise learn more from fools than fools learn from the wise."

CATO THE ELDER

APRIL 19

"Stop being afraid of what can go wrong and start being excited about what can go right."

UNKNOWN

APRIL 20

"If they tell you about the darkness of their life, then you are the light of their life."

UNKNOWN

APRIL 21

"Time is the wisest counselor of all."

PERICLES

APRIL 22

"To an optimist every weed is a flower, to a pessimist every flower is a weed"

FINNISH PROVERB

APRIL 23

"Remember, most of your stress comes from the way you respond, not the way life is. Adjust your attitude and all that extra stress is gone."

UNKNOWN

APRIL 24

"Gratitude is the wine for the soul. Go on. Get drunk."

RUMI

APRIL 25

"Change is the only constant in life."

HERACLITUS

APRIL 26

"The greatest strength is gentleness."

NATIVE AMERICAN PROVERB

APRIL 27

"Take risks. If you win you will be happy, if you lose you will be wise."

UNKNOWN

APRIL 28

"The only impossible journey is the one you never begin."

UNKNOWN

APRIL 29

"The greater the obstacle, the more glory in overcoming it."

MOLIÈRE

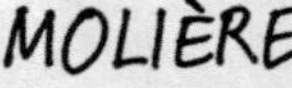

APRIL 30

"The unexamined life is not worth living."

SOCRATES

MAY 1

"Close the window that hurts you, no matter how beautiful the view is."

UNKNOWN

MAY 2

"Believe in your dreams, for they are the whispers of your soul urging you to pursue greatness."

UNKNOWN

MAY 3

"A silent man is the best one to listen to."

JAPANESE PROVERB

MAY 4

"In the middle of every difficulty lies opportunity."

ALBERT EINSTEIN

MAY 5

"Kindness is a gift everyone can afford to give."

UNKNOWN

MAY 6

"Every situation in life is temporary. So, when life is good, make sure you enjoy it fully. And when life is not so good, remember that it won't last forever and better days are on the way."

UNKNOWN

MAY 7

"Do not spoil what you have by desiring what you have not."

EPICURUS

MAY 8

"A thousand cups of wine do not suffice when true friends meet, but half a sentence is too much when there is no meeting of minds."

ANCIENT PROVERB

MAY 9

"If you can stay positive in a negative situation, you win."

UNKNOWN

MAY 10

"If it makes you happy it isn't a waste of time."

UNKNOWN

MAY 11

"Happiness is when what you think, what you say, and what you do are in harmony."

MAHATMA GANDHI

MAY 12

"The secret of change is to focus all your energy not on fighting the old but on building the new."

SOCRATES

MAY 13

"The most beautiful things in life are not things. They are people and places and memories and pictures. They are feelings and moments and smiles and laughter."

UNKNOWN

MAY 14

"Be an encourager. The world has plenty of critics already."

UNKNOWN

MAY 15

"Only a fool tests the depth of a river with both feet."

ASIAN PROVERB

MAY 16

"A man who fears suffering is already suffering from what he fears."

MONTAIGNE

MAY 17

"Sitting alone is better than walking with the wrong people."

UNKNOWN

MAY 18

"Wrong is wrong, even if everyone is doing it. Right is right, even if no one is doing it."

UNKNOWN

MAY 19

"Happiness depends upon ourselves."

ARISTOTLE

MAY 20

"A bird does not sing because it has an answer; it sings because it has a song."

NATIVE AMERICAN PROVERB

MAY 21

"Calmness is a human superpower. The ability not to overreact or take things personally keeps your mind clear and your heart at peace."

UNKNOWN

MAY 22

"Life becomes more meaningful when you realize the simple fact that you will never get the same moment twice."

UNKNOWN

MAY 23

"The fool doth think he is wise, but the wise man knows himself to be a fool."

WILLIAM SHAKESPEARE

MAY 24

"The happiness of your life depends upon the quality of your thoughts."

MARCUS AURELIUS

MAY 25

"A lot of what weighs you down isn't yours to carry."

UNKNOWN

MAY 26

"Hope is the belief that tomorrow will be better than today."

UNKNOWN

MAY 27

"Give a man a fish and you feed him for a day; teach a man to fish and you feed him for a lifetime."

ANCIENT PROVERB

MAY 28

"The doorstep to the temple of wisdom is a knowledge of our own ignorance."

BENJAMIN FRANKLIN

MAY 29

"In difficult times, true friends tell you the truth. In happy times, true friends celebrate with you. In sad times, true friends are by your side."

UNKNOWN

MAY 30

"Change in all things is sweet."

ARISTOTLE

MAY 31

"Stay kind, it makes you beautiful."

UNKNOWN

JUNE 1

"He who asks is a fool for five minutes, but he who does not ask remains a fool forever."

ANCIENT PROVERB

JUNE 2

"Make someone smile every day, but never forget that you are someone too."

UNKNOWN

JUNE 3

"It is rare to find someone that cares about you without another agenda. One that wants to see you achieve your dreams, encourages you to grow and is there through all your mess. Be grateful for those people in your life and always keep them close."

UNKNOWN

JUNE 4

"Contentment is the greatest wealth."

LAO TZU

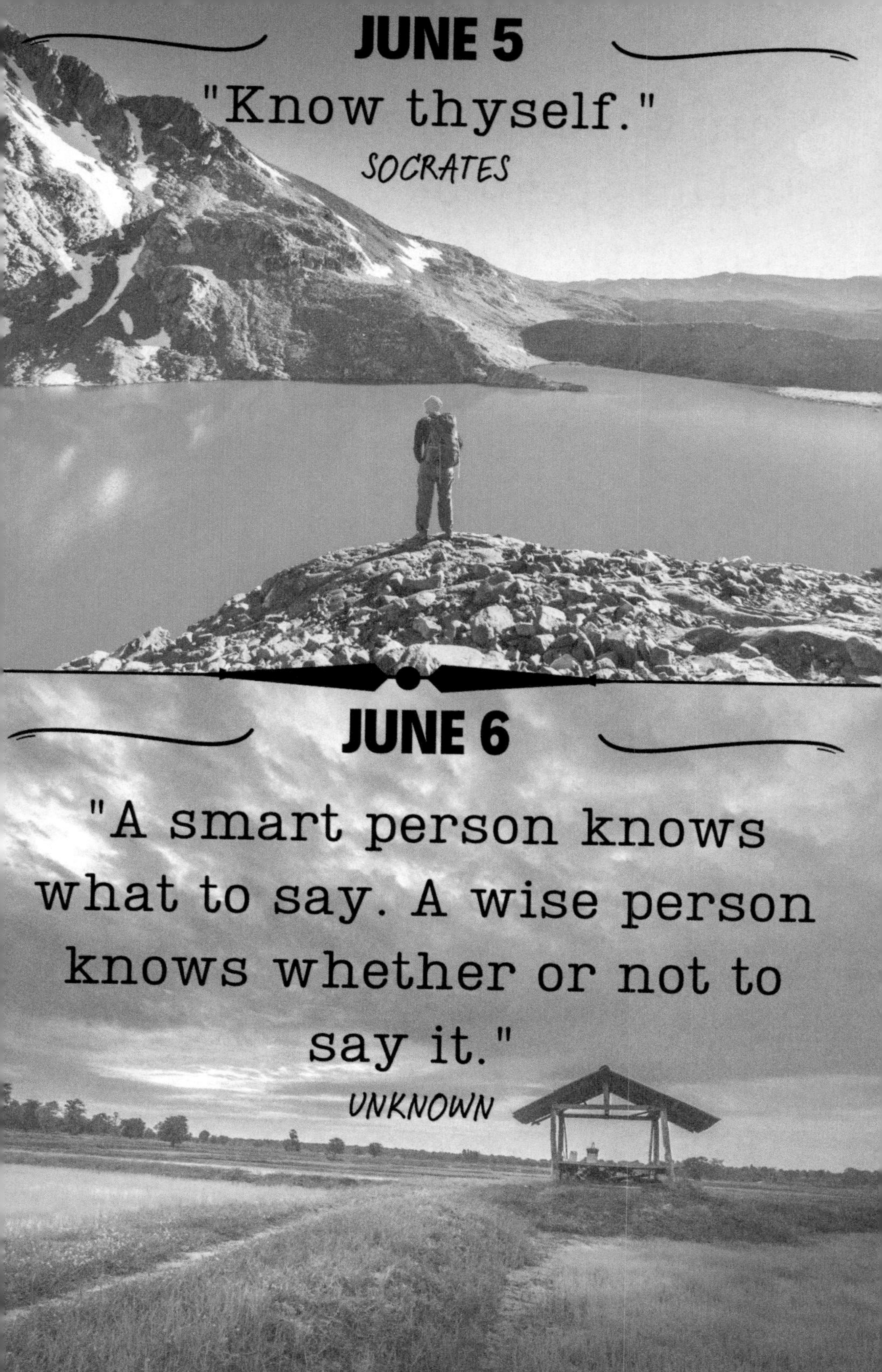

JUNE 5

"Know thyself."

SOCRATES

JUNE 6

"A smart person knows what to say. A wise person knows whether or not to say it."

UNKNOWN

JUNE 7

"Your hardest times often lead to the greatest moments of your life. Keep going. Tough situations build strong people in the end."

UNKNOWN

JUNE 8

"Don't be afraid to take a big step when one is indicated. You can't cross a chasm in two small jumps."

NATIVE AMERICAN PROVERB

JUNE 9

"Kindness is a language that the deaf can hear and the blind can see."

MARK TWAIN

JUNE 10

"Stay in your magic, no matter what."

UNKNOWN

JUNE 11

"Live less out of habit and more out of intent."

UNKNOWN

JUNE 12

"No man is free who cannot control himself."

PYTHAGORAS

JUNE 13

"A half-truth is a whole lie"

JEWISH PROVERB

JUNE 14

"The greatest act of encouragement is not to tell someone they can do it, but to help them realize it themselves."

UNKNOWN

JUNE 15

"It is better to travel hopefully, than to arrive disenchanted."

UNKNOWN

JUNE 16

"The weak can never forgive. Forgiveness is the attribute of the strong."

MAHATMA GANDHI

JUNE 17

"It is the mark of an educated mind to be able to entertain a thought without accepting it."

ARISTOTLE

JUNE 18

"It is better to let someone walk away from you than all over you."

UNKNOWN

JUNE 19

"If you focus on the hurt
you will continue to suffer.
If you focus on the lesson
you will continue to grow."

UNKNOWN

JUNE 20

"Turn your face
toward the sun,
and the shadows
fall behind you."

MAORI PROVERB

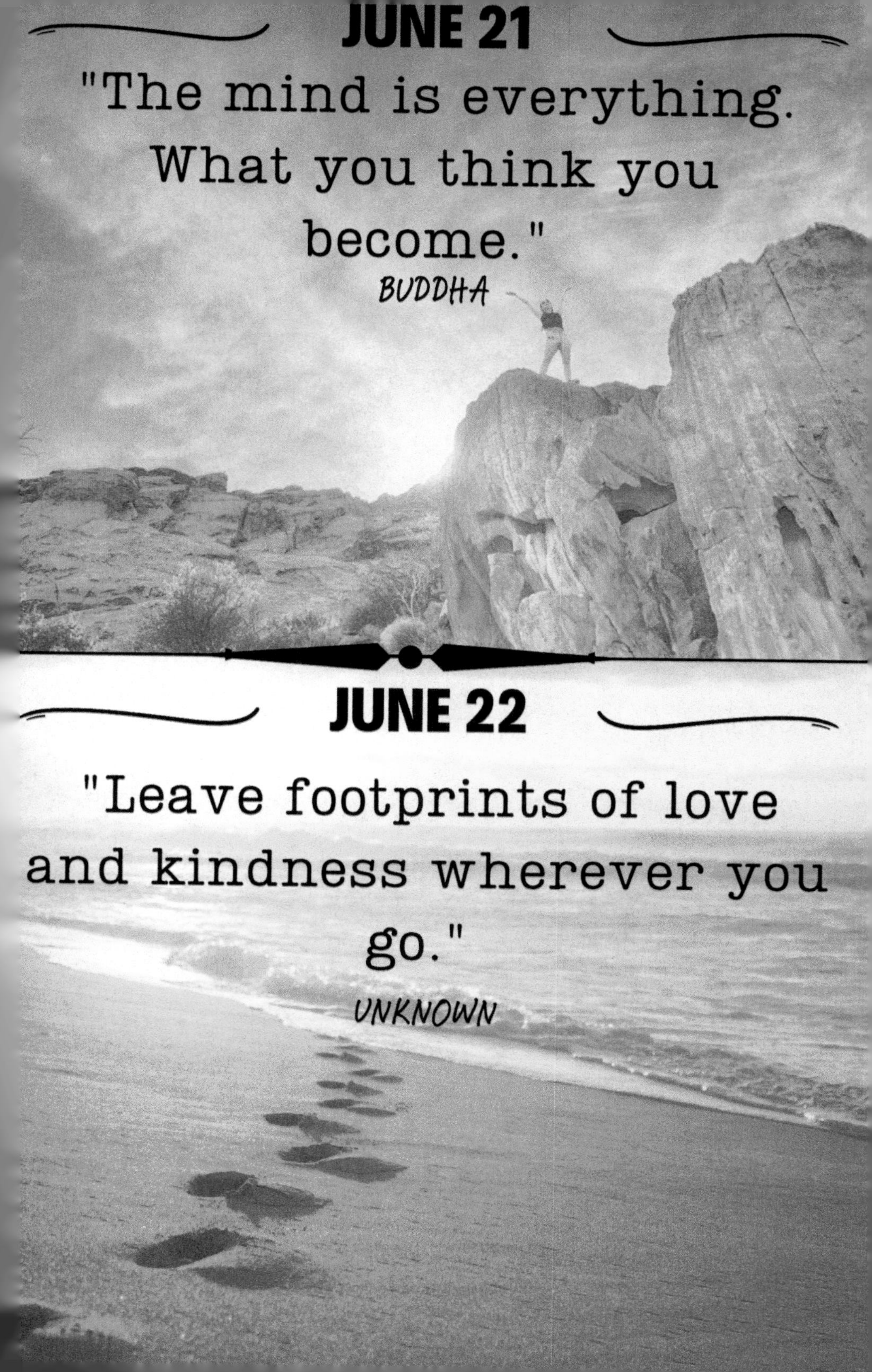

JUNE 21

"The mind is everything. What you think you become."

BUDDHA

JUNE 22

"Leave footprints of love and kindness wherever you go."

UNKNOWN

"Accept both compliments and criticism. It takes both sun and rain for a flower to grow."

UNKNOWN

JUNE 24

"Wisdom begins in wonder."

SOCRATES

JUNE 25

"Seek wisdom, not knowledge. Knowledge is of the past, wisdom is of the future."

NATIVE AMERICAN PROVERB

JUNE 26

"Don't limit your challenges. Challenge your limits."

UNKNOWN

JUNE 27

"Believe you can and you will."

UNKNOWN

JUNE 28

"Every great dream begins with a dreamer. Always remember, you have within you the strength, the patience, and the passion to reach for the stars to change the world."

HARRIET TUBMAN

JUNE 29

"The greatest wealth is to live content with little."

PLATO

JUNE 30

"Never underestimate the power of a kind word or a genuine compliment. It can change someone's entire day."

UNKNOWN

JULY 1

"The choices we make, the chances we take determine our destiny."

UNKNOWN

JULY 2

"The ones who are crazy enough to think they can change the world are the ones who do."

NATIVE AMERICAN PROVERB

"Success usually comes to those who are too busy to be looking for it."

HENRY DAVID THOREAU

JULY 4

"The person you took for granted today, may turn out to be the person you need tomorrow. Be careful how you treat people."

UNKNOWN

JULY 5

"Memories are always special. Sometimes we laugh when remembering the days we cried and sometimes we cry when we remember the days we laughed."

UNKNOWN

JULY 6

"The greatest way to live with honor in this world is to be what we pretend to be."

SOCRATES

JULY 7

"Failure can either destroy you or make you work ten times harder, it just depends on your mindset."

UNKNOWN

JULY 8

"Nothing is permanent. Don't stress yourself too much, because no matter how bad the situation seems, it will change."

UNKNOWN

JULY 9

"You can reinvent yourself as many times as you need."

UNKNOWN

JULY 10

"A roaring lion kills nothing."

AFRICAN PROVERB

JULY 11

"The dangers of life are infinite and among them is safety."

JOHANN WOLFGANG VON GOETHE

JULY 12

"Pay attention to who you are with when you are feeling your best."

UNKNOWN

JULY 13

"Some pursue happiness, others create it."

UNKNOWN

JULY 14

"It is not what happens to you, but how you react to it that matters."

EPICTETUS

JULY 15

"Before you let your voice be heard, first lick your lips."

INDONESIAN PROVERB

JULY 16

"When Plan A doesn't work, don't worry, you still have 25 more letters to go through."

UNKNOWN

JULY 17

"Never regret a day in your life. Good days bring you happiness and bad days give you experience."

UNKNOWN

JULY 18

"A man who cannot tolerate small misfortunes can never accomplish great things."

ANCIENT PROVERB

JULY 19

"It's not that I'm so smart, it's just that I stay with problems longer."

ALBERT EINSTEIN

JULY 20

"Trust takes years to build, seconds to break, and forever to repair."

UNKNOWN

JULY 21

"Train your mind and heart to see the good in everything. There is always something to be grateful for."

UNKNOWN

JULY 22

"Pleasure in the job puts perfection in the work."

ARISTOTLE

JULY 23

"A clear conscience is a soft pillow."

ANCIENT PROVERB

JULY 24

"Always find time for the things that make you feel happy to be alive."

UNKNOWN

JULY 25

"Always trust your instincts, they are messages from your soul."

UNKNOWN

JULY 26

"Respect is a mirror, the more you show it to other people, the more they will reflect it back."

NATIVE AMERICAN PROVERB

JULY 27

"The secret of happiness is not in doing what one likes, but in liking what one does."

JAMES M. BARRIE

JULY 28

"Everyone you meet has something to teach you."

UNKNOWN

JULY 29

"Words have the power to both destroy and heal. When words are both true and kind they can change our world."

UNKNOWN

JULY 30

"To find yourself, think for yourself."

SOCRATES

JULY 31

"A single conversation with a wise man is better than ten years of study."

ANCIENT PROVERB

AUGUST 1

"Thousands of candles can be lit from a single candle, and the life of the candle will not be shortened. Happiness never decreases by being shared."

UNKNOWN

AUGUST 2

"A soulmate is a friend who never leaves."

UNKNOWN

AUGUST 3

"One generation plants the trees; another gets the shade."

ANCIENT PROVERB

AUGUST 4

"If you can walk you can dance. If you can talk you can sing."

ZIMBABWEAN PROVERB

AUGUST 5

"Sometimes you think that you want to disappear, but all you really want is to be found."

UNKNOWN

AUGUST 6

"Whatever you believe about yourself on the inside is what you will manifest on the outside."

UNKNOWN

AUGUST 7

"Strength does not come from physical capacity. It comes from an indomitable will."

MAHATMA GANDHI

AUGUST 8

"Education is the kindling of a flame, not the filling of a vessel."

SOCRATES

AUGUST 9

"If it makes you happy, it doesn't have to make sense to others."

UNKNOWN

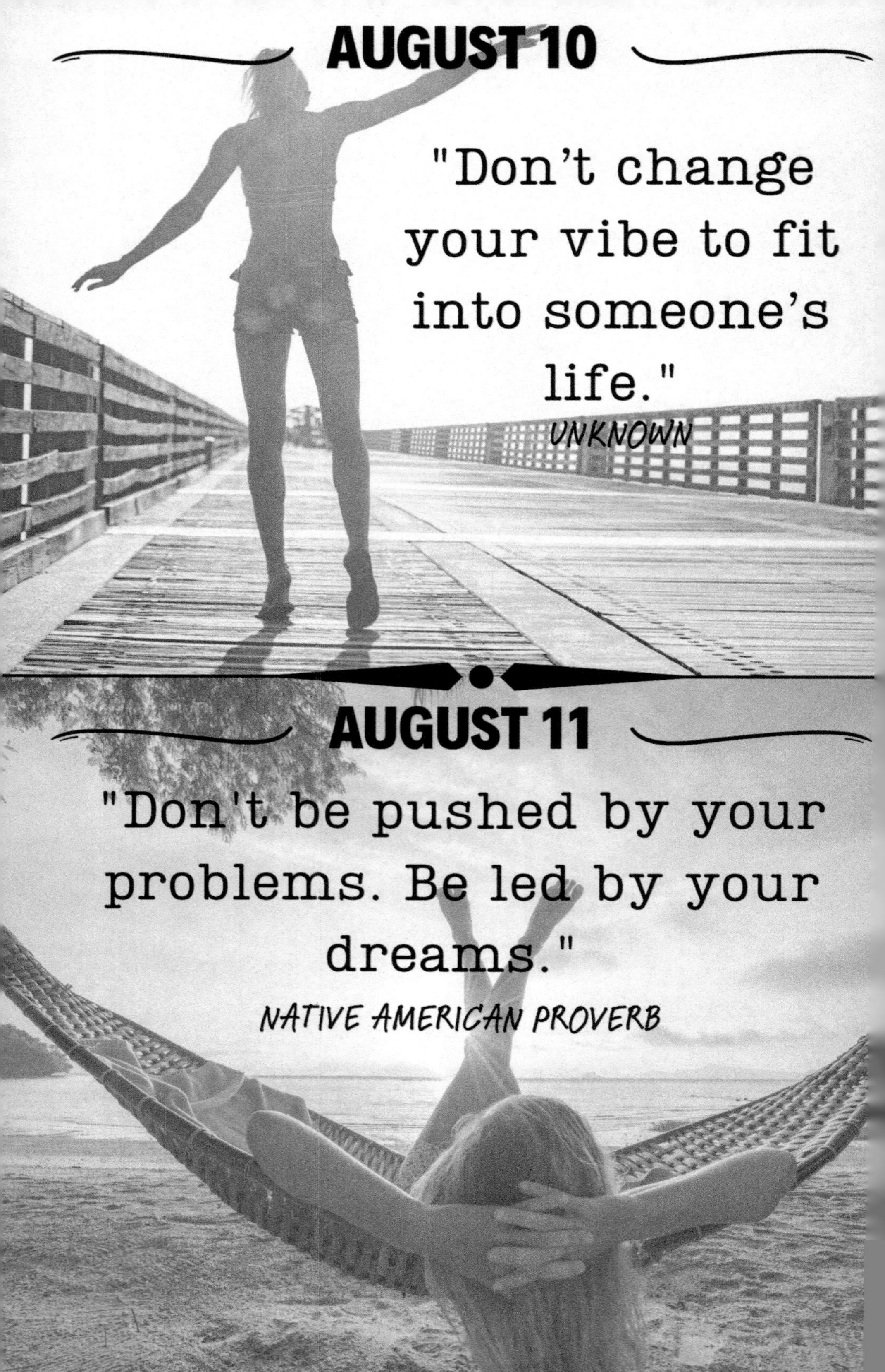

AUGUST 10

"Don't change your vibe to fit into someone's life."

UNKNOWN

AUGUST 11

"Don't be pushed by your problems. Be led by your dreams."

NATIVE AMERICAN PROVERB

AUGUST 12

"Many of life's failures are people who did not realize how close they were to success when they gave up."

THOMAS EDISON

AUGUST 13

"Imagine what you would do if you weren't afraid to fail?"

UNKNOWN

AUGUST 14

"A healthy mind does not speak ill of others."

UNKNOWN

AUGUST 15

"To understand everything is to forgive everything."

ANCIENT PROVERB

AUGUST 16

"Some men go through a forest and see no firewood."

ENGLISH PROVERB

AUGUST 17

"Stay close to people who feel like sunshine."

UNKNOWN

AUGUST 18

"The greatest gift you could give someone is your time. Because when you give your time, you are giving a portion of your life you can't get back."

UNKNOWN

AUGUST 19

"It is during our darkest moments that we must focus to see the light."

ARISTOTLE

AUGUST 20

"Patience is the key to paradise."

TURKISH PROVERB

AUGUST 21

"Time always exposes what you mean to someone."

UNKNOWN

AUGUST 22

"The pain you feel today is the strength you feel tomorrow."

UNKNOWN

AUGUST 23

"Your beliefs become your thoughts, your thoughts become your words, your words become your actions, your actions become your habits, your habits become your values, and your values become your destiny."

MAHATMA GANDHI

AUGUST 24

"Virtue is harmony."

PYTHAGORAS

AUGUST 25

"The essence of wisdom is to know when to speak your mind and when to mind your speech."

UNKNOWN

AUGUST 26

"Not everyone will understand your journey. That is fine. It is not their journey to make sense of, it is yours."

UNKNOWN

AUGUST 27

"A closed mind is like a closed book; just a block of wood."

ANCIENT PROVERB

AUGUST 28

"Peace comes from within. Do not seek it without."

BUDDHA

AUGUST 29

"Missing an opportunity because you lacked the courage to jump hurts more than trying and failing."

UNKNOWN

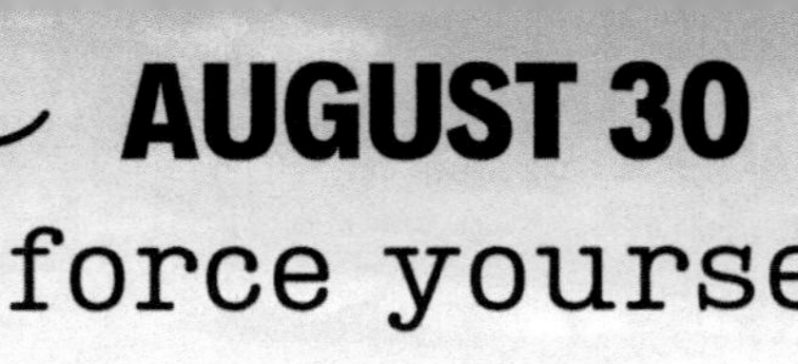

AUGUST 30

"Don't force yourself to fit in where you don't belong."

UNKNOWN

AUGUST 31

"A fall into a ditch makes you wiser."

ANCIENT PROVERB

SEPTEMBER 1

"The gem cannot be polished without friction, nor man perfected without trials."

CHINESE PROVERB

SEPTEMBER 2

"It is not what you say to others that determines your life. It is what you whisper to yourself that has the most power."

UNKNOWN

SEPTEMBER 3

"Sometimes we don't need advice, we just need somebody to listen."

UNKNOWN

SEPTEMBER 4

"Hope is the thing with feathers that perches in the soul and sings the tune without the words and never stops at all."

EMILY DICKINSON

SEPTEMBER 5

"It is better to have less thunder in the mouth and more lightning in the hand."

NATIVE AMERICAN PROVERB

SEPTEMBER 6

"We can never obtain peace in the outer world until we make peace with ourselves."

UNKNOWN

SEPTEMBER 7

"Beautiful souls recognize beautiful souls. Keep being genuine, your people will find you."

UNKNOWN

SEPTEMBER 8

"Ignorance, the root and stem of all evil."

PLATO

SEPTEMBER 9

"A wise man makes his own decisions, an ignorant man follows public opinion."

ANCIENT PROVERB

SEPTEMBER 10

"Look for something good in every day, even if some days you have to look a bit harder."

UNKNOWN

SEPTEMBER 11

"Don't let anyone who hasn't been in your shoes tell you how to tie your laces."

UNKNOWN

SEPTEMBER 12

"The successful person has the habit of doing the things failures don't like to do. They don't like doing them either necessarily. But their disliking is subordinated to the strength of their purpose."

E.M. GRAY

SEPTEMBER 13

"The person who removes a mountain begins by carrying away small stones."

ANCIENT PROVERB

SEPTEMBER 14

"If you feel like you're losing everything remember that trees lose their leaves every year and they still stand tall and wait for better days to come."

UNKNOWN

SEPTEMBER 15

"Always be careful when you follow the masses. Sometimes the "m" is silent."

UNKNOWN

SEPTEMBER 16

"If a man is proud of his wealth, he should not be praised until it is known how he employs it."

SOCRATES

SEPTEMBER 17

"The more you give, the more good things come to you."

NATIVE AMERICAN PROVERB

SEPTEMBER 18

"The ultimate value of life depends upon awareness and the power of contemplation, rather than the power of mere survival"

UNKNOWN

SEPTEMBER 19

"The next time someone tries to bring you down remember that confidence is quiet but insecurity is loud."

UNKNOWN

SEPTEMBER 20

"Discipline is choosing between what you want now and what you want most."

ABRAHAM LINCOLN

SEPTEMBE

"It is not enough

how to ride, you r

know how to fa

MEXICAN PROVERB

SEPTEMBER 22

"Words and hearts should be handled with care. Words when spoken and hearts when broken are the hardest things to repair."

UNKNOWN

EPTEMBER 23

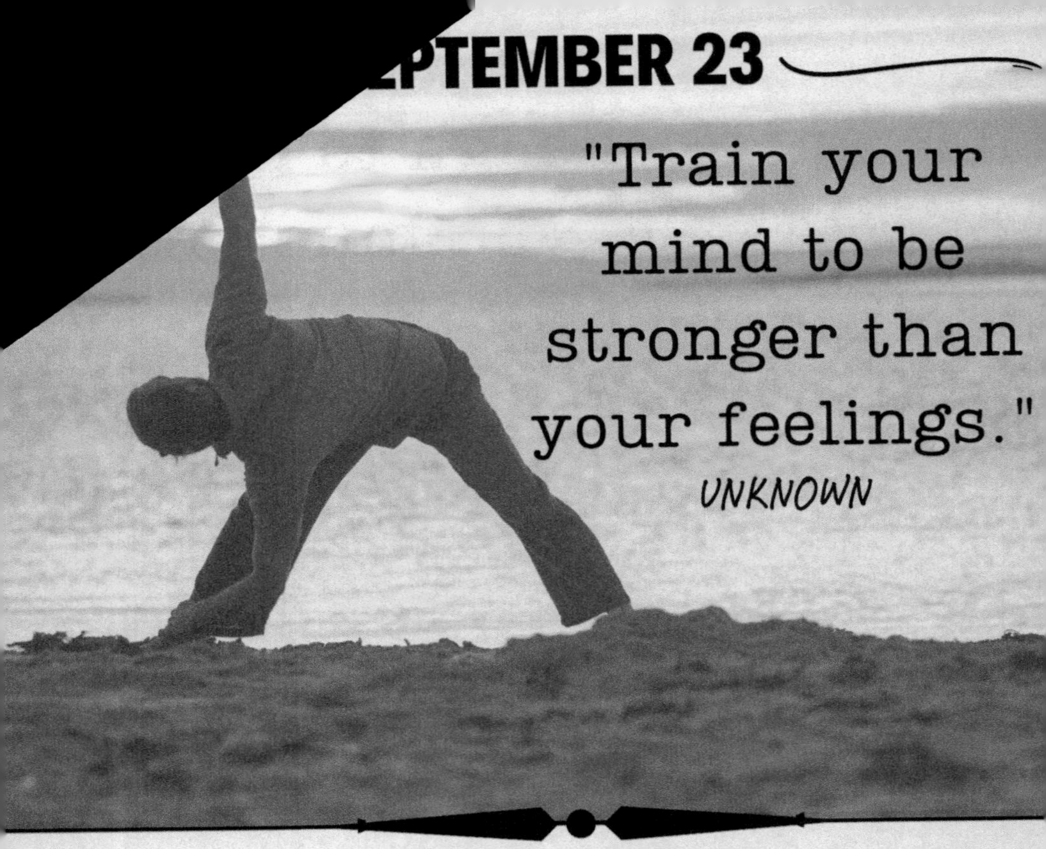

"Train your mind to be stronger than your feelings."

UNKNOWN

SEPTEMBER 24

"Happiness and freedom begin with a clear understanding of one principle: Some things are within our control, and some things are not."

EPICTETUS

SEPTEMBER 25

"The person who says it cannot be done should not interrupt the person doing it."

ANCIENT PROVERB

SEPTEMBER 26

"Don't waste your time looking back, you are not going that way."

UNKNOWN

SEPTEMBER 27

"People who defend your name when you are not around are the most loyal friends you could ever get."

UNKNOWN

SEPTEMBER 28

"The future belongs to those who believe in the beauty of their dreams."

ELEANOR ROOSEVELT

SEPTEMBER 29

"Don't be afraid of moving slowly; be afraid of standing still."

ANCIENT PROVERB

SEPTEMBER 30

"What people think about you is not important, what you think about yourself means everything."

UNKNOWN

OCTOBER 1

"Accept what you can't change. Change what you can't accept."

UNKNOWN

OCTOBER 2

"Good character, when established, is not easily overthrown by poverty or wealth."

HERODOTUS

OCTOBER 3

"For the beauty of the rose, we also water the thorns."

AFRICAN PROVERB

OCTOBER 4

"Dream it, wish it, do it."

UNKNOWN

OCTOBER 5

"Letting go of the past is your first step to happiness."

UNKNOWN

OCTOBER 6

"Empathy is seeing with the eyes of another, listening with the ears of another, and feeling with the heart of another."

ALFRED ADLER

OCTOBER 7

"There is no shame in not knowing, the shame lies in not finding out."

RUSSIAN PROVERB

OCTOBER 8

"Say no without guilt, say yes without fear."

UNKNOWN

OCTOBER 9

"Go where you feel most alive."

UNKNOWN

OCTOBER 10

"Love is composed of a single soul inhabiting two bodies."

ARISTOTLE

OCTOBER 11

"There are hundreds of paths up the mountain, all leading in the same direction, so it doesn't matter which path you take. The only one wasting time is the one who runs around and around the mountain telling everyone that his or her path is wrong."

HINDU PROVERB

OCTOBER 12

"You can't give your life more time, so give the time you have left more life."

UNKNOWN

OCTOBER 13

"Protect your heart from people who are not happy with themselves, they will never be happy with you."

UNKNOWN

OCTOBER 14

"Obstacles are those frightful things you see when you take your eyes off your goal."

HENRY FORD

OCTOBER 15

"If you can't live longer, live deeper."

ITALIAN PROVERB

OCTOBER 16

"When you know your worth, no one can make you feel worthless."

UNKNOWN

OCTOBER 17

"The belief in yourself must be stronger than those that don't believe in you."

UNKNOWN

OCTOBER 18

"You have power over your mind, not outside events. Realize this, and you will find strength."

MARCUS AURELIUS

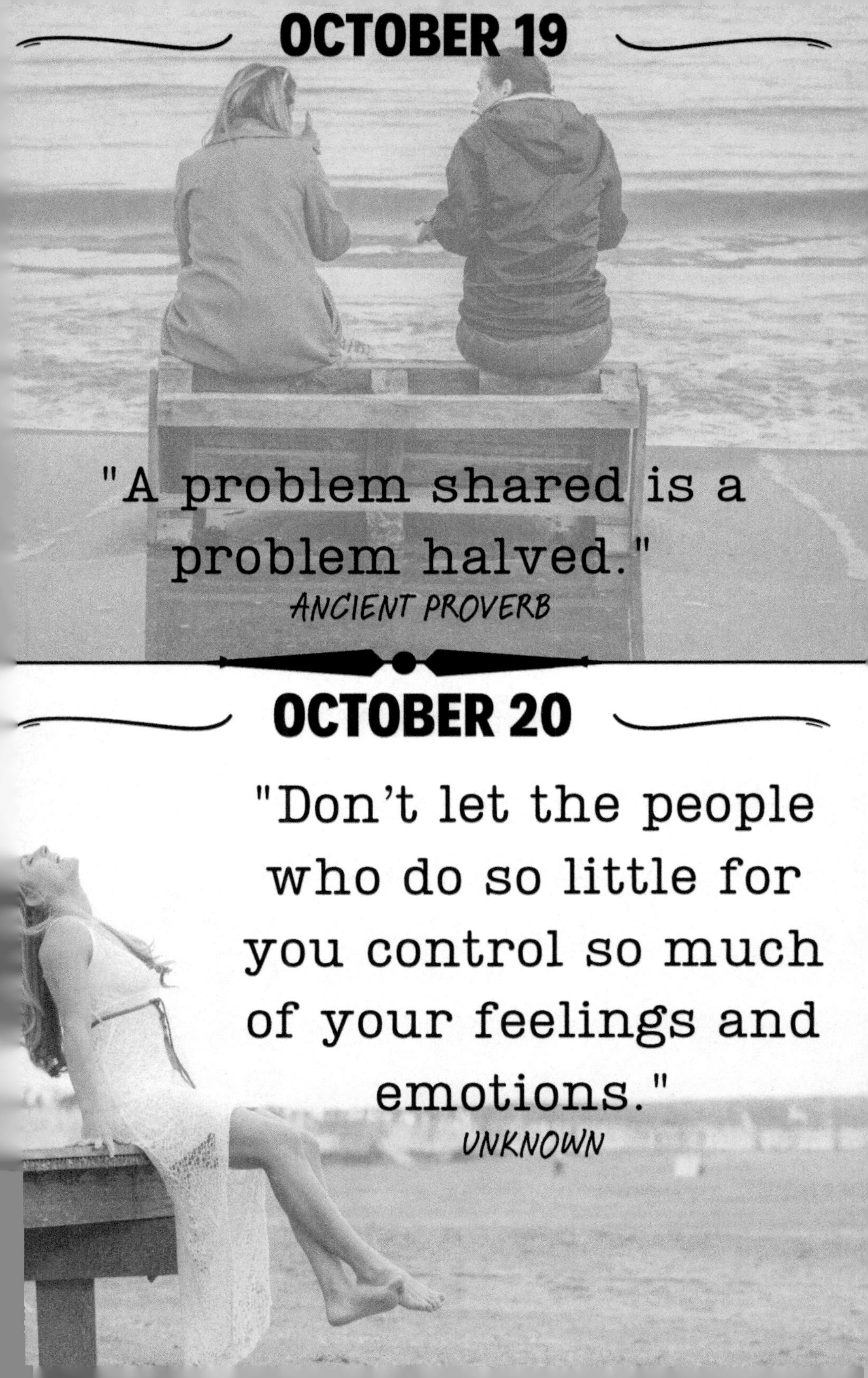

OCTOBER 19

"A problem shared is a problem halved."

ANCIENT PROVERB

OCTOBER 20

"Don't let the people who do so little for you control so much of your feelings and emotions."

UNKNOWN

OCTOBER 21

"One day you will leave your life behind, so live a life you will remember."

UNKNOWN

OCTOBER 22

"Believe you can and you're halfway there."

THEODORE ROOSEVELT

OCTOBER 23

"When anger rises, think first of the consequences."

ANCIENT PROVERB

OCTOBER 24

"A positive mind finds opportunity in everything. A negative mind finds fault in everything."

UNKNOWN

OCTOBER 25

"Correct a fool and he will hate you. Correct a wise man and he will appreciate you."

UNKNOWN

OCTOBER 26

"He who is not courageous enough to take risks will accomplish nothing in life."

NATIVE AMERICAN PROVERB

OCTOBER 27

"The way to gain a good reputation is to endeavor to be what you desire to appear."

SOCRATES

OCTOBER 28

"Don't waste energy hating people who hate you, spend it loving people who love you."

UNKNOWN

OCTOBER 29

"Never stop doing your best just because someone doesn't give you credit."

UNKNOWN

OCTOBER 30

"Character is like pregnancy, it cannot be hidden forever."

AFRICAN PROVERB

OCTOBER 31

"When the tree falls, the monkeys scatter."

ANCIENT PROVERB

NOVEMBER 1

"Stop shrinking yourself to fit places you've outgrown."

UNKNOWN

NOVEMBER 2

"Happiness is a choice not a result. Nothing will make you happy until you choose to be happy."

UNKNOWN

NOVEMBER 3

"Happiness does not come from happiness itself, but from the journey towards achieving it."

FINNISH PROVERB

NOVEMBER 4

"A single tree cannot make a forest."

ANCIENT PROVERB

NOVEMBER 5

"Be who you want to be, not what others want to see."

UNKNOWN

NOVEMBER 6
"Do everything with a good heart and expect nothing in return."
UNKNOWN
NOVEMBER 7
"The secret of getting ahead is getting started."
MARK TWAIN

NOVEMBER 8

"Patience is a bitter plant, but it has sweet fruit."

ANCIENT PROVERB

NOVEMBER 9

"You don't have to control your thoughts, you just have to stop letting them control you."

DAN MILLMAN

NOVEMBER 10

"You live most of your life inside of your head. Make sure it's a nice place to be."

UNKNOWN

NOVEMBER 11

"Listen to the wind, it talks. Listen to the silence, it speaks. Listen to your heart, it knows."

NATIVE AMERICAN PROVERB

NOVEMBER 12

"Do not remove a fly from your friend's forehead with a hatchet."

ANCIENT PROVERB

NOVEMBER 13

"You can't go back and change the beginning, but you can start where you are and change the ending."

UNKNOWN

NOVEMBER 14

"Stop trying so hard to be liked by everyone, because you don't even like everyone."

UNKNOWN

NOVEMBER 15

"The only person you are destined to become is the person you decide to be."

RALPH WALDO EMERSON

NOVEMBER 16

"Don't worry that others don't know you; worry that you don't know yourself."

ANCIENT PROVERB

NOVEMBER 17

"The way you make others feel about themselves says a lot about you."

UNKNOWN

NOVEMBER 18

"More powerful than the will to win is the courage to begin."

UNKNOWN

NOVEMBER 19

"The highest reach of injustice is to be deemed just when you are not."

PLATO

NOVEMBER 20

"Tell me, and I'll forget. Show me, and I may remember. Involve me, and I'll understand."

ANCIENT PROVERB

NOVEMBER 21

"If you love yourself it doesn't matter if other people don't like you because you don't need their approval to feel good about yourself."

UNKNOWN

NOVEMBER 22

"Nothing is stronger than a broken person rebuilding themselves."

UNKNOWN

NOVEMBER 23

""Teachers open the door, but you must enter by yourself."

ANCIENT PROVERB

NOVEMBER 24

"Hope is the companion of power and the mother of success; for those who hope strongly have within them the gift of miracles."

SAMUEL SMILES

NOVEMBER 25

"Never miss out on a good person that can make your life great just because they're a little difficult. The good ones never come easy."

UNKNOWN

NOVEMBER 26

"A satisfied life is better than a successful life, because a successful life is measured by others, but our satisfaction is measured by own our soul, mind and heart."

UNKNOWN

NOVEMBER 27

"When the winds of change blow, some people build walls and others build windmills."

GAELIC PROVERB

NOVEMBER 28

"Truth is more valuable if it takes you a few years to find it."

FRENCH PROVERB

NOVEMBER 29

"The sign of a beautiful person is that they always see beauty in others."

UNKNOWN

NOVEMBER 30

"Don't be perfect, be real."

UNKNOWN

DECEMBER 1

"There are three solutions to every problem: accept it, change it, or leave it. If you can't accept it, change it. If you can't change it, leave it."

BUDDHA

DECEMBER 2

"You grow differently when you have good people with good intentions in your life."

UNKNOWN

DECEMBER 3

"A great attitude becomes a great day, which becomes a great month, which becomes a great year, which becomes a great life."

UNKNOWN

DECEMBER 4

"Never wait for a perfect moment. Just take a moment and make it perfect."

UNKNOWN

DECEMBER 5

"Opportunity is missed by most people because it is dressed in overalls and looks like work."

THOMAS EDISON

DECEMBER 6

"Be not disturbed at being misunderstood; be disturbed rather at not being understanding."

ANCIENT PROVERB

DECEMBER 7

"The more you love your decisions, the less you need others to love them."

UNKNOWN

DECEMBER 8

"Never cry for the person that hurts you, just smile and say thank you for giving me a chance to find someone better than you."

UNKNOWN

DECEMBER 9

"You will not be the same person a year from now, but you must decide which way you will grow."

UNKNOWN

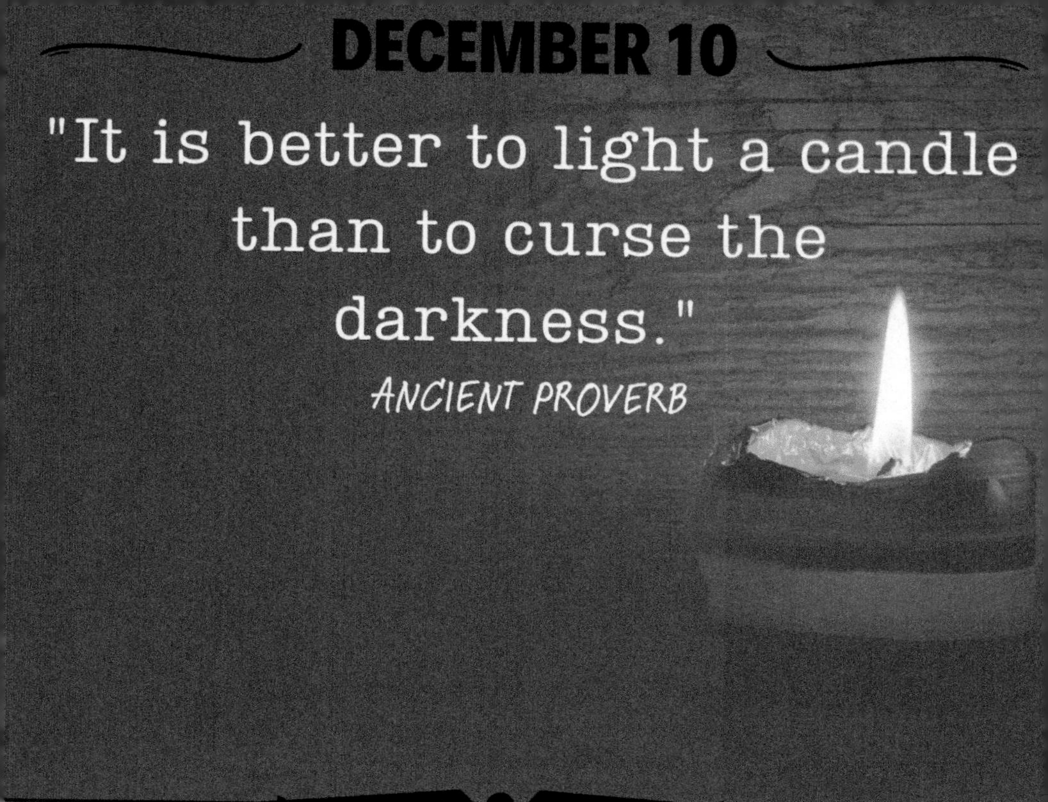

DECEMBER 10

"It is better to light a candle than to curse the darkness."

ANCIENT PROVERB

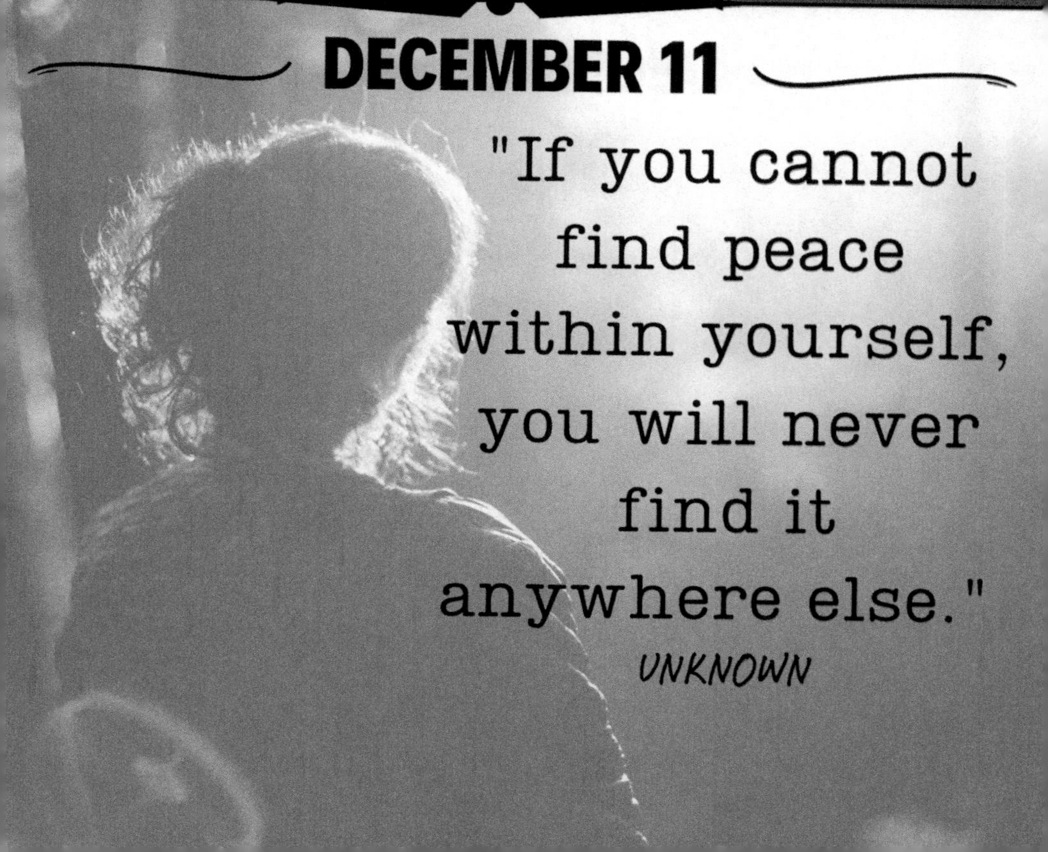

DECEMBER 11

"If you cannot find peace within yourself, you will never find it anywhere else."

UNKNOWN

DECEMBER 12

"Each day is another chance to change your life."

UNKNOWN

DECEMBER 13

"Focus on the step in front of you, not the whole staircase."

ANCIENT PROVERB

DECEMBER 14

"There are two things you should never waste your time on: things that don't matter and people who think that you don't matter."

UNKNOWN

DECEMBER 15

"Kindness is a gift that everyone can afford to give."

UNKNOWN

DECEMBER 16

"Don't judge my choices when you don't understand my reasons."

UNKNOWN

DECEMBER 17

"Some of the sweetest berries grow among the sharpest thorns."

GAELIC PROVERB

DECEMBER 18

"Stop being the one who makes all the effort. Sit back and let the ship sink."

UNKNOWN

DECEMBER 19

"If you don't fight for what you want, don't cry for what you lost."

UNKNOWN

DECEMBER 20

"It's OK to outgrow people who don't grow. Grow tall anyways."

UNKNOWN

DECEMBER 21

"The tree with the most leaves will not necessarily produce juicy fruit."

BRAZILIAN PROVERB

DECEMBER 22

"The less you respond to negativity the more peaceful your life will become."

UNKNOWN

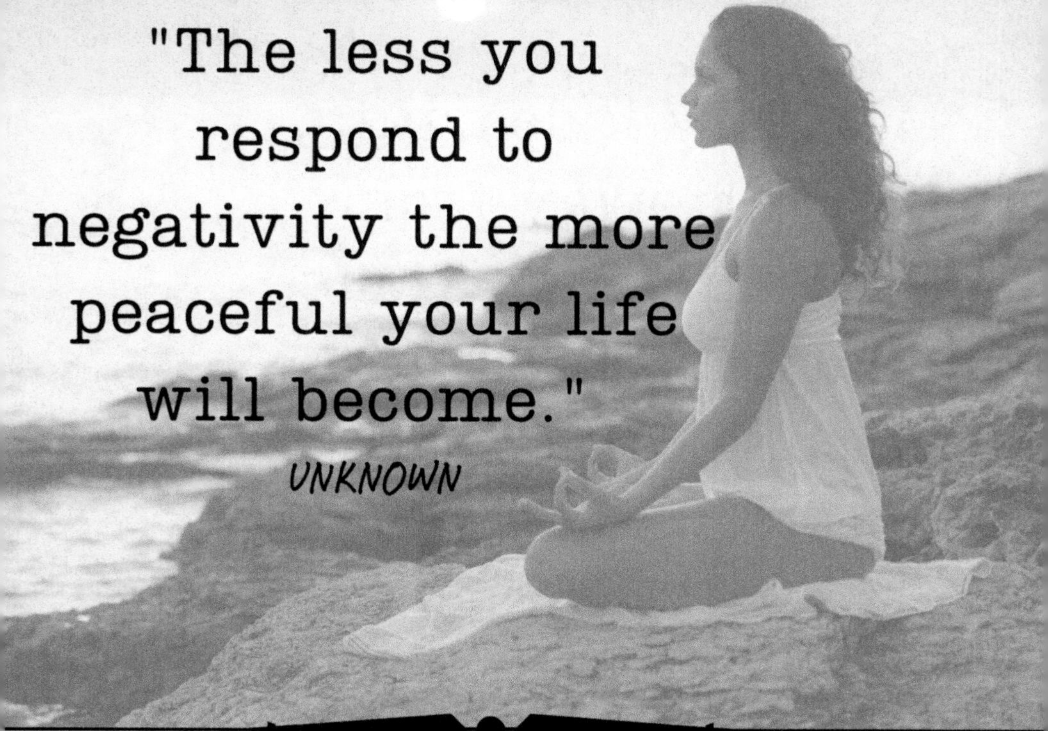

DECEMBER 23

"Overthinking does nothing but kill your happiness."

UNKNOWN

DECEMBER 24

"Maturity is learning to walk away from people and situations that threaten your piece of mind, self-respect, values, morals or self worth."

UNKNOWN

DECEMBER 25

"That is the simple secret of happiness. Whatever you are doing, don't let the past move your mind and don't let the future disturb you. Because the past is no more, and the future is not yet."

BUDDHA

DECEMBER 26

"Two things define you: your patience when you have nothing and your attitude when you have everything."

UNKNOWN

DECEMBER 27

"You become a master of your life when you learn how to control where your attention goes. Value what you give your energy to."

UNKNOWN

DECEMBER 28

"Never forget who was there for you when no one else was."

UNKNOWN

DECEMBER 29

"If you are patient in one moment of anger, you will escape a hundred days of sorrow."

ANCIENT PROVERB

DECEMBER 30

"If you're the smartest person in the room, you're in the wrong room."

UNKNOWN

DECEMBER 31

"We don't grow when things are easy, we grow when we face challenges."

UNKNOWN

Printed in Great Britain
by Amazon

33139823R00106